Women &
Leadership

SpiritBuilt Leadership 10

Malcolm Webber

Published by:

Strategic Press
www.StrategicPress.org

Strategic Press is a division of Strategic Global Assistance, Inc.
www.sgai.org

513 S. Main St. Suite 2
Elkhart, IN 46516
U.S.A.

+1-844-532-3371 (LEADER-1)

ISBN 978-1-888810-42-4

All Scripture references are from the New International Version of the Bible, unless otherwise noted.

Printed in the United States of America

Table of Contents

Introduction

The role of women in ministry and leadership in the church is a very controversial issue about which much has been written.

We can identify two major *extremes* of teaching and practice:

- In some circles, women are not allowed to occupy any position of leadership or fulfill any formal ministry in the church – except for those involving children or other women. This teaching holds that women are simply never called by God to leadership; leadership is exclusively a male domain.
- In other circles, women are commonly found in the very highest positions of authority. This teaching maintains that one should find as many women as men in leadership roles including the very top positions – leadership is a 50/50 proposition when it comes to gender.

Of course, between these two extremes are many shades and nuances.

Furthermore, emotions run high on this matter – on both sides. It is an extremely important issue that directly affects everyone in the church.

In this study we will examine what the Bible says about the role of women in Christian ministry and leadership.[1]

Malcolm Webber, Ph.D.
Elkhart, Indiana
December, 2004

---

[1] Our discussion will be limited to women and leadership. We will not deal with a woman's specific roles as wife and mother; that is done extensively in *The Christian Family* by Malcolm Webber.

Chapter 1

Two Fundamental Affirmations

Before dealing directly with the subject of women and leadership in the Bible, we must first make two fundamental, biblical affirmations regarding gender:

1. The Bible affirms that men and women are equal.
2. The Bible affirms that men and women are different.

Men and Women Are Equal

Our first fundamental affirmation is that men and women are equal.

This is not to say that there are no legitimate distinctions between men and women, but that men and women are fundamentally equal in the eyes of God. From the time of creation, men and women have been equal.

We were created equally in God's image:

> *So God created man in his own image, in the image of God he created him; male and female he created them. (Gen. 1:27)*

Men and women were equally given authority over the earth:

> *God blessed them and said to them, "Be fruitful and increase in number; fill the earth and subdue it. Rule over the fish of the sea and the birds of the air and over every living creature that moves on the ground." (Gen. 1:28)*

Outside of Christ, men and women are equally sinful and lost, and in need of a Savior. Neither is uniquely responsible for the other's sins. Moreover, in Christ, both men and women receive the same eternal life and righteousness before God through faith by Jesus' shed blood.

> *This righteousness from God comes through faith in Jesus Christ to all who believe. There is no difference, for all have sinned and fall short of the glory of God, and are justified freely by his grace through the redemption that came by Christ Jesus. (Rom. 3:22-24)*

Men and women are equally valuable in the sight of God. He loves them both and desires to save them both:

> *And believers were the more added to the Lord, multitudes both of men and women. (Acts 5:14)*

> *But when they believed Philip preaching the things concerning the kingdom of God, and the name of Jesus Christ, they were baptized, both men and women. (Acts 8:12)*

Both Christian men and women are equally saved through the shed blood of Jesus by the power of the Holy Spirit who transforms us into the same image of Jesus Christ:

> *You are all sons of God through faith in Christ Jesus, for all of you who were baptized into Christ have clothed yourselves with Christ. There is neither Jew nor Greek, slave nor free, male nor female, for you are all one in Christ Jesus. (Gal. 3:26-28)*

In Christ, men and women are "one." This does not deny male-female distinctions but affirms that we are equally accepted by God and welcome in His presence, equally able to grow by the power of the Holy Spirit into maturity.

There are no mediators between God and man other than Jesus (1 Tim. 2:5). Thus, the husband does not mediate between Jesus and his wife or between Jesus and his children. All can, and must, go to Jesus directly. Moreover, the man will not judge his wife and children on the Last Day. Jesus, alone, is the Judge; we're all directly accountable to Him.

Men are not more inclined than women to be godly, and the profile of spiritual maturity for both male and female is the same list of character qualities: love, joy, peace, patience, kindness, goodness, faithfulness, gentleness and self-control (Gal. 5:22-23).

Christian men and women have equal access to God, and should live equally in the presence of the Holy Spirit. Men and women are called equally to know God, to love Him, to obey Him and to serve Him. We equally possess calling and purpose from God (2 Tim. 1:9) and we are equally gifted by God to fulfill our callings (Rom. 12:3-6; 1 Cor. 12:7).

God has given an important ministry to every man and woman; therefore, we must all serve Him and fulfill His purpose for our lives – not only the men.

Men and Women Are Different

As we have seen, men and women are equal. However, we are also different. This is our second biblical affirmation.

That men and women are profoundly different in many ways is a self-evident truth. Someone who refuses to acknowledge that is deeply committed to irrationality.

> The erasure of distinctions between the sexes is not only the most striking issue of our time, it may be the most profound the race has ever confronted. (William Manchester, historian)

Men and women are equal but different. Consequently, there are distinctions in our roles in the family and in the church.

Now I want you to realize that the head of every man is Christ, and the head of the woman is man, and the head of Christ is God. (1 Cor. 11:3)

This does not make the woman inferior to the man any more than Christ should be considered inferior to the Father simply because in the order of the Godhead He is subject to His Father. Jesus and His Father are "One" (John 10:30); they are equal. Yet they are different; they have different roles within the Godhead.

Peter gives the balance in 1 Peter 3:7:

Husbands, in the same way be considerate as you live with your wives, and treat them with respect as the weaker partner and as heirs with you of the gracious gift of life, so that nothing will hinder your prayers. (1 Pet. 3:7)

In this verse, "heirs with you" could have been translated as "joint-heirs." Thus, men and women are *different* ("weaker partner"[2]) but they are *equal* heirs of life in Christ. Consider these different translations of the same verse:

...She may be weaker than you are, but she is your equal partner in God's gift of new life... (New Living Translation)

...bestowing honor on the woman as the weaker sex, since you are joint heirs of the grace of life... (Revised Standard Version)

...as with a weaker, [even] the female, vessel, giving [them] honour, as also fellow-heirs of [the] grace of life... (Darby translation)

...the weaker vessel, as being also joint-heirs of the grace of life... (American Standard Version)

---

[2] By "weaker," Peter refers to comparative physical (not spiritual) weakness. Also the husband is often "stronger" economically and in other ways.

Peter affirms both: God created us fundamentally *equal* but also fundamentally *different* with different gender roles.

This was God's design. This is not something that was unwise or inappropriate. It was God's wise design that we should be equal but different.

God could have created everyone male or everyone female. He could have designed a reproductive process that only needed one gender so that humanity would endure and multiply. But He did not do so. He intentionally made men and women different so they could each fulfill their different purposes. That was wise of God to do so, and it is wise of us to recognize that reality.

The Relationship of Father and Son in the Godhead

Equality of value does not necessarily mean identical roles and functions. In a parallel concept, the members of the triune Godhead are equal:

> *I and the Father are one. (John 10:30)*

> *… he was even calling God his own Father, making himself equal with God. (John 5:18)*

> *For in Christ all the fullness of the Deity lives in bodily form, (Col. 2:9)*

Yet they possess distinct functions:

> *who have been chosen according to the foreknowledge of God the Father, through the sanctifying work of the Spirit, for obedience to Jesus Christ and sprinkling by his blood… (1 Pet. 1:2)*

Thus, the Father is said to be the "Head" of Christ[3]:

> *Now I want you to realize that ...the head of Christ is God. (1 Cor. 11:3)*

This is order within the Godhead. This is difference of role and function. This does not make Jesus a "second rate deity" or mean that He is being discriminated against! Moreover, Jesus is quite content in His role. He does not covet His Father's ultimate authority.

Paul intentionally uses the relationship of Father and Son in the Godhead as a picture of the relationship between husband and wife:

> *Now I want you to realize that the head of every man is Christ, and the head of the woman is man, and the head of Christ is God. (1 Cor. 11:3)*

Thus, while the Bible teaches the fundamental equality of men and women, it does not teach the uniformity of their roles. We are equal before God but we have different roles. Moreover, these roles are all important. We all have significant ministry giftings and callings. We all have significant responsibilities that we need to fulfill.

What is most important is that we each fulfill our callings in God, rather than competing with each other for what we perceive as the "most important" calling.

The role of leadership may appear to some to be "more important," but, in reality, what is most important is that we all fulfill the particular will of God for our lives.

> *Nevertheless, each one should retain the place in life that the Lord assigned to him and to which God has called him. This is the rule I lay down in all the churches. Was a man already circumcised when*

---

[3] In this same sense, Jesus said "the Father is *greater* than I" (John 14:28). This was an expression of His submission to His Father, not of any intrinsically lesser value.

he was called? He should not become uncircumcised. Was a man uncircumcised when he was called? He should not be circumcised. Circumcision is nothing and uncircumcision is nothing. Keeping God's commands is what counts. Each one should remain in the situation which he was in when God called him. Were you a slave when you were called? Don't let it trouble you – although if you can gain your freedom, do so. For he who was a slave when he was called by the Lord is the Lord's freedman; similarly, he who was a free man when he was called is Christ's slave. You were bought at a price; do not become slaves of men. Brothers, each man, as responsible to God, should remain in the situation God called him to. (1 Cor. 7:17-24)

God created men and women to be different and to have different roles and functions. This is how God did it. It is not merely some human tradition.

We are all equal before God, but we do not have the same roles or functions. We each have important callings, but those callings are not the same – any more than our physical, mental or emotional make-ups are the same. Men and women are very different; that's the way God made us. Consequently, we have different functions in the family and in the church.

The Need for Balance

Men and women are equal yet different. Our theology must be big enough to embrace both of these truths.

Any theology that overemphasizes one of these truths will be imbalanced. Those who overemphasize "equal" end up having no distinctions at all, and losing the power of distinctly male leadership in the home and church.

Conversely, those who overemphasize "different" end up with the women doing very little in the church by way of ministry. Moreover, some women become bound with a fear of "getting out of their place," while others become angry and resentful.

15

Too much "equal" ➜	Men don't lead as they should. The family and the church are robbed.
	Women try to fulfill roles they are not properly equipped for.

Too much "difference" ➜	Men become authoritarian masters treating the women more as slaves than as equal heirs of God's grace.
	Some women become passive and do not fulfill God's purposes; others become angry and resentful. The family and the church are robbed.

We must keep a balance: men and women are equal yet different.

With these two realities in mind, let's now look at what the Bible teaches regarding leadership and ministry in the church as relates to gender.

A Holistic Approach

Our approach will not be to try to find some quick "proof-texts" to prove a certain view. Rather, we will endeavor to be true to the broad realities of teaching across the scope of the entire Bible.

There are three broad biblical realities that we will now examine:

1. God has established male leadership in the family and church.
2. Women do minister and lead in the Bible.
3. Women are not in the top positions of leadership as often as men.

Chapter 2

God Has Established Male Leadership

The Bible clearly teaches that God has established male leadership in the family and in the church. This is evident from a number of things.

1. At creation, God made man to be the primary leader.

   > *The Lord God said, "It is not good for the man to be alone. I will make a helper suitable for him" (Gen. 2:18)*

   God's purpose in creating woman was for her to "help" man. That does not make her "less," just different.

   Thus, God established the man as the primary leader. This means that the man is the one who should take responsibility for establishing the vision and defining the goals – with the woman's help of course. Then she works with him, "helping" him, in the fulfilling of God's call – for the family and for the church.

   The fact that God created Adam first is, in itself, a statement of male leadership:

   > *A woman should learn in quietness and full submission. I do not permit a woman to teach or to have authority over a man; she must be silent. For Adam was formed first, then Eve. (1 Tim. 2:11-13)*

Without, at this point, going into everything that Paul did or did not mean in this passage,[4] it is obvious that one of Paul's justifications of male leadership here is the fact that Adam was created first.

2.   The prominent leaders in the Old Testament were almost all men.

There were very few exceptions to this. There were some wonderful women in the Old Testament, but the prominent leaders were male.

3.   The Levitical priests were all men. It was not possible for a woman to be a priest. That was God's ordination. This also made Israel considerably different from the nations around her, who commonly had priestesses in their religions.

4.   Nearly all the rulers of Israel were men. There were two exceptions to this. First, there was Deborah, a godly woman who led Israel to victory (Jud. 4:4). Second, there was Athaliah, who usurped the throne with violence (2 Kings 11; 2 Chron. 22-24).

5.   Nearly all the national prophets were men.

Certainly there were some prominent women in the Old Testament but we do see the principle of male leadership firmly established in Israel by God.

Then in the New Testament we find the same thing:

1.   Jesus was a Man. He came to be King – so He didn't come as a woman but as a man.

And just as we have borne the likeness of the earthly man, so shall we bear the likeness of the man from heaven. (1 Cor. 15:59)

---

[4] In Chapter 5, we will do this.

18

2. Jesus' top leadership team was composed entirely of men.

> *These are the names of the twelve apostles: first, Simon (who is called Peter) and his brother Andrew; James son of Zebedee, and his brother John; Philip and Bartholomew; Thomas and Matthew the tax collector; James son of Alphaeus, and Thaddaeus; Simon the Zealot and Judas Iscariot, who betrayed him. (Matt. 10:2-4)*

So we see that Jesus Himself practiced the idea of "different." However, Jesus certainly treated women as equal to men. He saved women, He healed women, He delivered women from oppression, He taught women – just as much as He did men. Women had access to Him, just as much as men did. Women traveled with Him, and ministered to Him (Luke 8:3[5]; Mark 15:41). Women were as valuable in His eyes as men. He died for women just as much as He died for men.

Yet when Jesus chose His top leadership team, He chose twelve men – not six men and six women!

3. The epistles teach different roles for men and women, emphasizing male leadership responsibility in the home and in the church.

> *Now I want you to realize that the head of every man is Christ, and the head of the woman is man, and the head of Christ is God. (1 Cor. 11:3)*

> *As in all the congregations of the saints, women should remain silent in the churches. They are not allowed to speak, but must be in submission, as the Law says. If they*

---

[5] At this time, although women were allowed to hear the teaching of the Scriptures in the synagogues, they were not allowed to be disciples of a rabbi. For a Jewish woman to leave home and travel with a rabbi was not only unheard of, it was scandalous. Thus, Luke 8:3 is a significant affirmation of women!

want to inquire about something, they should ask their own husbands at home; for it is disgraceful for a woman to speak in the church. (1 Cor. 14:34-35)

Now as the church submits to Christ, so also wives should submit to their husbands in everything. (Eph. 5:24)

Wives, submit to your husbands, as is fitting in the Lord. (Col. 3:18)

That the wife is to "submit" to her husband does not mean:

- The wife is inferior.
- The wife is to be passive or surrender all independent thought.
- The wife is to do absolutely everything the husband demands.
- The wife is to mindlessly enable her husband's sin and irresponsibility.
- The husband is to stifle his wife's creativity or gifts.
- The husband is allowed to oppress or abuse his wife.[6]

Then they can train the younger women to love their husbands and children, to be self-controlled and pure, to be busy at home, to be kind, and to be subject to their husbands, so that no one will malign the word of God. (Tit. 2:4-5)

A woman should learn in quietness and full submission. I do not permit a woman to teach or to have authority over a man; she must be silent. For Adam was formed first, then Eve. (1 Tim. 2:11-13)

Here is a trustworthy saying: If anyone sets his heart on being an overseer, he desires a noble task. Now the overseer

---

[6] For more on the specific roles of husband and wife, and the nature of godly submission please see *The Christian Family* by Malcolm Webber.

must be above reproach, the husband of but one wife... (1 Tim. 3:1-2)

He must manage his own family well and see that his children obey him with proper respect. (If anyone does not know how to manage his own family, how can he take care of God's church?) (1 Tim. 3:4-5)

These are clear affirmations of male primary leadership in the church and home. Authority over the children resides in the father. Of course, the mother also has authority over the children, but the father is the leader.

An elder must be blameless, the husband of but one wife, a man whose children believe and are not open to the charge of being wild and disobedient. (Tit. 1:6)

Wives, in the same way be submissive to your husbands so that, if any of them do not believe the word, they may be won over without words by the behavior of their wives, when they see the purity and reverence of your lives. Your beauty should not come from outward adornment, such as braided hair and the wearing of gold jewelry and fine clothes. Instead, it should be that of your inner self, the unfading beauty of a gentle and quiet spirit, which is of great worth in God's sight. For this is the way the holy women of the past who put their hope in God used to make themselves beautiful. They were submissive to their own husbands, like Sarah, who obeyed Abraham and called him her master. You are her daughters if you do what is right and do not give way to fear. (1 Pet. 3:1-6)

So, it is clear that God has given the man the primary leadership responsibility – in the home and in the church.

But does this mean that women can never lead? Does this mean that women have no ministry in the church, apart from that involving children and other women?

We now come to our second major point: it is also an inescapable fact that women *do* minister and lead in the Bible.

Chapter 3

Women Do Minister and Lead in the Bible

In the previous chapter, we saw that God has established male leadership in the home and church. Within this primary context, there are many biblical examples of women ministering and leading to the fullest extent of their callings in God.

We can see this in many ways:

1. THE OLD TESTAMENT.

There are some prominent (albeit rare) Old Testament examples of women in leadership of various kinds:

> *Then Miriam the prophetess, Aaron's sister, took a tambourine in her hand, and all the women followed her, with tambourines and dancing. (Ex. 15:20)*

Miriam functioned as a "prophetess" in Israel; this was her formal ministry office.

> *They made the bronze basin and its bronze stand from the mirrors of the women who served at the entrance to the Tent of Meeting. (Ex. 38:8)*

Apparently, these were women of character and influence in Israel who had some kind of ministry role at the Tabernacle.

Deborah, a prophetess, the wife of Lappidoth, was leading Israel at that time.... Village life in Israel ceased, ceased until I, Deborah, arose, arose a mother in Israel. (Jud. 4:4; 5:7)

Deborah functioned as the very top leader in Israel. This is the exception that proves the rule of male leadership, but it's still an exception.

So Joab sent someone to Tekoa and had a wise woman brought from there... (2 Sam. 14:2)

In Israel, there was a particular group of people who were recognized in the community for their wisdom. This group of people devoted themselves not only to gaining wisdom but also to teaching others how to gain it. These wisdom instructors were simply called "wise men" (e.g., Jer. 18:18) and "wise women" (2 Sam. 14:2), and they functioned as teacher-counselors to those who sought their wisdom. These teachers taught their pupils wise attitudes and lifestyles, just as they would their own children (cf. Gen. 45:8; Jud. 5:7; Prov. 5:1). Significantly, their number included women.

The following three passages reveal the existence of "prophetesses" in Israel. In the first passage, the male leaders sought the Word of the Lord through the prophetess, on behalf of the king:

Hilkiah the priest, Ahikam, Acbor, Shaphan and Asaiah went to speak to the prophetess Huldah... (2 Kings 22:14)

Then I went to the prophetess, and she conceived and gave birth to a son. And the Lord said to me, "Name him Maher-Shalal-Hash-Baz." (Is. 8:3)

There was also a prophetess, Anna... (Luke 2:36)

For a dynamic portrayal of a mighty woman, please read Proverbs 31:10-31. The woman described here is a mover and a shaker! She's an aggressive woman. She's involved in business and conducts trade. She runs her own household and gives instruction to others. She functions very assertively in her community. She's not afraid to do things for fear of someone accusing her of being "out of order."

> *And afterward, I will pour out my Spirit on all people. Your sons and daughters will prophesy, your old men will dream dreams, your young men will see visions. Even on my servants, both men and women, I will pour out my Spirit in those days. (Joel 2:28-29)*

Clearly, the Holy Spirit wants to anoint both men and women to function supernaturally.

2. THE GOSPELS.

Significantly, the first evangelist in the New Testament was a Samaritan woman:

> *Just then his disciples returned and were surprised to find him talking with a woman. But no one asked, "What do you want?" or "Why are you talking with her?" Then, leaving her water jar, the woman went back to the town and said to the people, "Come, see a man who told me everything I ever did. Could this be the Christ?" They came out of the town and made their way toward him. (John 4:27-30)*

Moreover, the gospel of Jesus' resurrection was proclaimed to men for the very first time by a woman (Mary Magdalene) at the command of Jesus Himself!

Jesus said, "Do not hold on to me, for I have not yet returned to the Father. Go instead to my brothers and tell them, 'I am returning to my Father and your Father, to my God and your God.'" Mary Magdalene went to the disciples with the news: "I have seen the Lord!" And she told them that he had said these things to her. (John 20:17-18)

3. THE PRACTICES OF THE EARLY CHURCH.

There are numerous examples in Acts and the epistles of women functioning in ministry and leadership roles:

He began to speak boldly in the synagogue. When Priscilla and Aquila heard him, they invited him to their home and explained to him the way of God more adequately. (Acts 18:26)

Significantly the Greek verb "explained" is plural. "They" (both Priscilla and Aquila) taught Apollos, not just Aquila.

He had four unmarried daughters who prophesied. (Acts 21:9)

Doubtless Philip's daughters prophesied publicly to the whole church and not only privately or to women and children alone.

I commend to you our sister Phoebe, a servant of the church in Cenchrea. I ask you to receive her in the Lord in a way worthy of the saints and to give her any help she may need from you, for she has been a great help to many people, including me. (Rom. 16:1-2)

In verse 1, Phoebe is called a "servant" of the church. This word could be understood as signifying "deaconess" and is translated that way by some Greek authorities (such as Alford). In any case, she was certainly a worker at the church there. Consider these other translations of the same verse:

> But I commend to you Phoebe, our sister, who is minister of the assembly which is in Cenchrea; (Darby Translation)

> And I commend you to Phebe our sister – being a ministrant of the assembly that [is] in Cenchrea (Young's Literal Translation)

> Our sister Phoebe, a deacon in the church in Cenchrea, will be coming to see you soon. (New Living Translation)

Moreover, Phoebe was probably the one who carried Paul's letter to the saints at Rome. So Paul trusted her with a high degree of responsibility.

> Greet Priscilla and Aquila, my fellow workers in Christ Jesus. (Rom. 16:3)

In Romans 16:3, Paul calls Priscilla and Aquila his "fellow workers in Christ," and he even names Priscilla first, possibly indicating her greater note as a Christian worker. Significantly, the word "workers" is plural. Paul considered Priscilla his "fellow worker." The context is Christian ministry; Paul is not referring here to the tent-making trade, which both he and they shared.

> I plead with Euodia and I plead with Syntyche to agree with each other in the Lord. Yes, and I ask you, loyal yokefellow, help these women who have contended at my side in the cause of the gospel, along with Clement and the rest of my fellow workers, whose names are in the book of life. (Phil. 4:2-3)

Apparently, these two women, Euodia and Syntyche, were on Paul's apostolic team.[7] Paul says they "have contended at my side in the cause of the gospel" and he calls them "my fellow workers."

> *Do your best to get here before winter. Eubulus greets you, and so do Pudens, Linus, Claudia and all the brothers. (2 Tim. 4:21)*

In 2 Timothy 4:21, Paul greets Timothy on behalf of several Roman Christians. The four named are quite likely leaders in Rome, since early Christian tradition (Irenaeus, *Against Heresies* 3:3) names Linus as the bishop of Rome. Significantly, "Claudia" is a woman's name – apparently she is one of the key leaders in the church at Rome.

> *On the Sabbath we went outside the city gate to the river, where we expected to find a place of prayer. We sat down and began to speak to the women who had gathered there. One of those listening was a woman named Lydia, a dealer in purple cloth from the city of Thyatira, who was a worshiper of God. The Lord opened her heart to respond to Paul's message. When she and the members of her household were baptized, she invited us to her home. "If you consider me a believer in the Lord," she said, "come and stay at my house." And she persuaded us. (Acts 16:13-15)*

Acts 16 indicates that, at her conversion, Lydia became the benefactor both of Paul's apostolic team and of the embryonic Christian community in Philippi. That meant she was also a leader in the church, since heads of households usually assumed the same role in the church that was centered in that household.

---

[7] For an excellent commentary on this passage, please see Appendix 1: Gordon Fee's Commentary on Philippians 4:2-3.

My brothers, some from Chloe's household have informed me that there are quarrels among you. (1 Cor. 1:11)

Paul wrote literally that he was told about the Corinthians "by those of Chloe." Here was a woman who had some authority – whether it was her family spoken of here or she was a busineswoman and sent her workers to Paul to tell him what was happening in the Corinthian church, we don't know. But she was recognized by Paul as having some kind of leadership responsibility and authority.

So I counsel younger widows to marry, to have children, to manage their homes and to give the enemy no opportunity for slander. (1 Tim. 5:14)

Thus, it is the responsibility of the wife and mother to "manage" the home. That does not make her the primary leader of the home, but it does give her responsibility and authority.

4. PAUL'S INSTRUCTIONS.

Since Paul gives specific instructions regarding women ministering in the church it must have been acceptable to him for women to function in the church's life. Here are some examples of this:

And every woman who prays or prophesies with her head uncovered dishonors her head... (1 Cor. 11:5)

The context of 1 Corinthians 11 is the public meeting of the believers. In that public meeting, apparently it is acceptable to Paul for women to take the position of temporary "leadership" that publicly praying or prophesying entails. It is unlikely that Paul is talking about group prayer here (everyone praying at the same time), but a woman leading in prayer. Similarly, to prophesy in a public meeting is to lead at that point. Obviously this is not a long-term "primary" leadership role in the church, but it is assertive ministry.

In 1 Timothy 3, Paul gives instructions to a certain group of women about how to conduct their lives and ministries in the church:

> *In the same way, their wives are to be women worthy of respect, not malicious talkers but temperate and trustworthy in everything. (1 Tim. 3:11)*

In the English translation, the words "their wives" indicate that Paul is addressing the wives of the deacons, following his instructions regarding deacons in verses 8-10. However, in the original Greek text, the word "their" is not found. The text reads simply "wives." Moreover, scholars are divided as to whether this refers to the deacons' wives or to a specific group of "deaconesses," since the Greek word can mean either "wife" or "woman." Since there is no Greek word for "deaconess,"[8] Paul may have referred here to women who serve the church in some formal ministry capacity.[9]

Here is one last passage that reveals Paul's intention for women:

> *Likewise, teach the older women to be reverent in the way they live, not to be slanderers or addicted to much wine, but to teach what is good. Then they can train the younger women to love their husbands and children, (Tit. 2:3-4)*

---

[8] Rom. 16:1 uses the same Greek word as "deacon" in 1 Tim. 3 and Phil. 1:1.

[9] In defense of the meaning "deaconesses": (1) the introductory phrase "in the same way," which is characteristic of exhortation to distinct groups, (2) the exact replication of verses 8-10's sentence structure in verse 11 and (3) the dependence of each verse on the initial "must" verb of the passage in verse 2, make a reference to women deacons equally possible. Significantly, the Chinese Bible simply translates this as "deaconess"; this is one reason why there are so many women ministering in the Chinese churches.

These passages all demonstrate that Paul expected women to minister in the church and to lead. This is not in the sense of taking over the responsibility of primary leadership; however, within the context of primary male leadership, women are clearly expected to minister and lead to the fullest extent of their callings in God. This is why Paul gives them instructions on how to minister appropriately – just as he gives the men instructions on how to minister appropriately.

5. THE PRINCIPLES OF EARLY CHURCH LIFE.

The New Testament teaches that men and women are both gifted by God and called into significant ministry in the church.

> For by the grace given me I say to every one of you: Do not think of yourself more highly than you ought, but rather think of yourself with sober judgment, in accordance with the measure of faith God has given you. Just as each of us has one body with many members, and these members do not all have the same function, so in Christ we who are many form one body, and each member belongs to all the others. We have different gifts, according to the grace given us. If a man's gift is prophesying, let him use it in proportion to his faith. If it is serving, let him serve; if it is teaching, let him teach; if it is encouraging, let him encourage; if it is contributing to the needs of others, let him give generously; if it is leadership, let him govern diligently; if it is showing mercy, let him do it cheerfully. (Rom. 12:3-8)

> Now to each one the manifestation of the Spirit is given for the common good. (1 Cor. 12:7)

> What then shall we say, brothers? When you come together, everyone has a hymn, or a word of instruction,

a revelation, a tongue or an interpretation. All of these must be done for the strengthening of the church. (1 Cor. 14:26)

Each one should use whatever gift he has received to serve others, faithfully administering God's grace in its various forms. If anyone speaks, he should do it as one speaking the very words of God. If anyone serves, he should do it with the strength God provides, so that in all things God may be praised through Jesus Christ... (1 Pet. 4:10-11)

This is a general principle of healthy church life – everyone, including all the women, should minister and function.

This does not mean that we all do the same things or that everyone should be ultimately "in charge" – obviously that would result in confusion. But everyone should function and minister. Then the church is healthy.

Just as the definition of a healthy physical body is that every part of the body functions properly, so the definition of a healthy church is that every member functions properly. Moreover, just as the members of the physical body are all significant though having different roles to play, so it is in the church.

Just as God has called and gifted the men to function and serve in the life and ministry of the church, so He has called the women to function and serve in the life and ministry of the church.

Thus, we see that the Bible contains both teaching and examples of women ministering and leading to the fullest extent of their callings in God.

A church that denies women the opportunity to minister has robbed itself of at least one-half of the gifts and callings God has provided.

But while we do see abundant evidence of women leading and ministering in a healthy spiritual community, we do not see much evidence of
women in the very *top* positions of leadership.

Chapter 4

"Top" Leadership

In the Bible, women are not in the top positions of leadership as often as men. An honest reading of the Scriptures will acknowledge this.

For example, there is only *one* Deborah in the entire Old Testament. With this one exception, the rulers of Israel – including Moses, Joshua, the Judges, the kings, Ezra, Nehemiah, etc. – were all men.

Furthermore, in Deborah's time, there were indications that this condition of top female leadership was not necessarily the best (cf. Is. 3:12). It appears that the men – in the following case, Barak – were not fulfilling their responsibilities in God.

> *Deborah, a prophetess, the wife of Lappidoth, was leading Israel at that time. She held court under the Palm of Deborah between Ramah and Bethel in the hill country of Ephraim, and the Israelites came to her to have their disputes decided. She sent for Barak son of Abinoam from Kedesh in Naphtali and said to him, "The LORD, the God of Israel, commands you: 'Go, take with you ten thousand men of Naphtali and Zebulun and lead the way to Mount Tabor. I will lure Sisera, the commander of Jabin's army, with his chariots and his troops to the Kishon River and give him into your hands.'" Barak said to her, "If you go with me, I will go; but if you don't go with me, I won't go." "Very well," Deborah said, "I will go with you. But because of the way you are going about this, the honor will not be yours, for the LORD will hand Sisera over to a woman."... (Jud. 4:4-9)*

In the New Testament, there were no women included in Jesus' twelve apostles. In many ways, Jesus went far beyond His time and culture in the manner in which He honored women; He treated both men and women with equality. However, if His intention had been to promote the idea of a 50/50 male-female split at the very top levels of leadership, this would have been the perfect way to make that point, and He declined to do so. His top leadership team consisted entirely of men.

Similarly, in the days of the Early Church, while we recognize the vibrant role of women in ministry – including, as we have noted, being a part of Paul's apostolic team as well as other leadership teams – there are few examples of women as "top" leaders.

To speak this way is not at all to undermine the idea of "equality." Some people believe that in a church that recognizes the "full equality" of men and women, half the top leaders must necessarily be female. Such a position cannot be defended from Scripture.

If we simply read the Bible from cover to cover, we will not come away with the position that half of its top leaders are female. There are few female top leaders in the Bible. Certainly there are some notable ones, just as there have been some great women God has used throughout history in top leadership roles.[10] But it is not half.

Equality does not mean a 50/50 proposition. Equality means that we genuinely value and truly integrate the feminine characteristics of humanity into our families, our churches and our ministries. Equality also means that both male and female have the opportunity to be all that God has called them and gifted them to be. In many ways, this does represent a major transformation that must be made in our thinking and in our churches; traditionally, women have been suppressed in many churches. But, when such a change of thinking is accomplished, there will still be more male top leaders than female ones. That is simply the way God has made humanity (1 Cor. 11:3).

---

[10] For example, see *Daughters of the Church* by Ruth A. Tucker and Walter Liefeld for a lengthy study of the prominent role of women from New Testament times to the present.

Two Streams of Thought

One basic principle of biblical interpretation is that we should not build a doctrine on isolated texts, but instead we should build our doctrines on the major streams of thought in Scripture and then interpret the isolated texts in light of those doctrines.

Therefore, as we strive to come to a balanced biblical perspective on the role of women in leadership, we should avoid the temptation to rely solely on Scriptures such as 1 Corinthians 14:34-35 and 1 Timothy 2:11-15 (which seem to forbid any kind of female ministry or authority in the church) on the one hand, or Galatians 3:28 (which seems to promote an entire leveling of all gender distinctions as they relate to authority and responsibility) on the other. We will examine these three passages of Scripture in the next chapter.

As we have seen, in the Bible there are two main streams of thought on the subject of women and leadership:

1. God has given men primary leadership responsibility and authority in the home and church.
2. Women should minister and lead to the fullest extent of their divine callings.

These two core ideas should provide the basis for the development of our doctrine on women and leadership. We should build our doctrine on the major biblical streams of thought and practice, and then interpret the occasional difficult proof-text in view of that – and not vice-versa!

So, how do we resolve these two streams of thought? Is there any contradiction between them or can they coexist?

A Resolution

In seeking a balanced resolution to this controversial issue, we believe in male leadership in the family and church (consistent with the biblical affirmations of such), *and* in women ministering and leading to the fullest extent of their callings in God (consistent with the biblical affirmations of such).

Much of the controversy over this issue can be resolved simply by realizing that there are many different *levels* of authority, leadership and ministry.

Biblically, the *ultimate* leader in family and church should be male (consistent with the way God made mankind). On many occasions, godly male leadership will bring stability, balance and protection from deception. However, within that context of primary male leadership, women should minister and lead to the fullest extent of their giftings, callings and purposes in God.

We see this pattern in the home. The father is the ultimate authority in the home, but the mother has authority when he's not around – certainly the male children are not above their mother in authority! That the mother does have authority in the home is clearly taught and practiced in the Bible (e.g., Eph. 6:1, "children, obey your parents"). Moreover, when the father assumes primary responsibility for leadership, this will bring security and stability to the home, and will, in fact, empower the mother's authority.[11]

We see this same pattern in Paul's apostolic team. As we saw from Philippians 4:2-3 as well as in the case of Priscilla and others, Paul had women on his apostolic team. Yet, clearly Paul was the leader of the team. The women ministered with initiative and responsibility, but they did so in the context of ultimate male authority.

---

[11] When a wife and mother is widowed and has no male relatives to assist her with raising her children, the brothers in the church should take godly responsibility for helping to lead that family.

This is a balanced resolution of the whole teaching of Scripture: the ultimate leadership in the church and family is male, and within that context, women should lead and minister to the fullest extent of their callings in God.

Are There Ever Exceptions?

Is it possible that God could raise up a Deborah who would be the *final* authority in a church or ministry? Of course this is possible – particularly if there are no men around who have the courage to take the final responsibility.[12] It is easy to simply say, "No women in positions of top leadership, only men!" But what if there are no men who are willing or competent to do so?

Of course God can raise up a woman as a top leader. He did it once in Israel. It was God who established Deborah; she didn't raise herself up. Moreover, God has done this throughout church history – particularly in many mission fields historically and even today. The men would not go and God sent the women. In any case, God can do what He wants – irrespective of our position on women and leadership!

But does this happen often? Biblically, it does not.

---

[12] Some Christian teachers promote the idea that if the man is not willing or competent to assume the appropriate leadership role in the home or church, the woman should be passive and allow the work to fail rather than step in and take the lead. This idea is not biblical (e.g., 1 Sam. 25; Acts 4:18-20; 5:29). Praise God for women who do have the courage and strength to take spiritual responsibility at home and in the church, rather than simply letting their families and churches fail! Of course, at the same time, they should not nag their husbands but rather pray that God will raise the men up to assume their leadership responsibilities and as soon as they begin to do so, the women should encourage them and begin gently to give the leadership back to them.

In summary, the biblical balance is:

- The *ultimate* leader in family and church should be male (consistent with the way God made mankind).

- Within that context of primary male leadership, women should minister and lead to the fullest extent of their giftings, callings and purposes in God.

This balanced position effectively reflects the whole complex teaching of the Scripture and not merely one or two simplistic proof-texts.

Chapter 5

Avoiding the Extremes

Men and women are equal yet different. As we noted earlier, there are two extremes of teaching on the subject of women and leadership:

- The "equal" extreme.
- The "different" extreme.

After briefly looking at each extreme, we will examine the biblical passages that are used most commonly to support them.

The "Equal" Extreme

Here is an example of the "equal" extreme:[13]

> The new covenant in Christ, whereby there is "neither male nor female," does away completely with any sort of male priesthood or spiritual chain of command within marriage.

> If women and men are equally capable of discerning and implementing God's will, then a woman does not need a man to exercise spiritual authority over her.

The basis for this position is found in Galatians 3:

> *There is neither Jew nor Greek, slave nor free, male nor female, for you are all one in Christ Jesus. (Gal. 3:28)*

---

[13] No references or names will be given for any of the following quotes, since our intention is not to criticize their authors.

At first glance, this verse seems to indicate a New Testament leveling of all gender distinctions as they relate to authority and responsibility. Men appear to hold no unique role of leadership or authority.

However, one must examine the entire context of this verse. As we study Galatians 3:1 – 4:7 we can easily see that Paul is not dealing with male-female issues in leadership and ministry, but he deals specifically with the question of salvation; this is the obvious theme of the entire book of Galatians.

False teachers, the Judaizers, had infiltrated the new churches at Galatia, teaching that the Gentile believers had to be circumcised and obey the Law of Moses to be saved (cf. Acts 15:1). Paul's purpose in his letter to the Galatians is to refute this false gospel:

> *I am astonished that you are so quickly deserting the one who called you by the grace of Christ and are turning to a different gospel – which is really no gospel at all. Evidently some people are throwing you into confusion and are trying to pervert the gospel of Christ. But even if we or an angel from heaven should preach a gospel other than the one we preached to you, let him be eternally condemned! (Gal. 1:6-8)*

It is in this context that Galatians 3:28 is written. It comes in the midst of Paul's discussion of God's covenant of grace with Abraham, the purpose of the Law of Moses, and justification in Christ by faith apart from the Law. Paul's point in Galatians 3:28 is that the distinctions between Jew and Gentile, slave and freeman, male and female are totally irrelevant when it comes to receiving salvation by God's grace. It is faith in Christ that makes the difference regardless of one's race, social status, gender or whether or not one has been circumcised.

Before the revelation of God's grace in Jesus Christ, salvation had been offered only to the Jews:

> *Therefore, remember that formerly you who are Gentiles by birth and called "uncircumcised" by those who call themselves "the circu-*

mcision" (that done in the body by the hands of men) – remember that at that time you were separate from Christ, excluded from citizenship in Israel and foreigners to the covenants of the promise, without hope and without God in the world. (Eph. 2:11-12; see also Ps. 147:19-20; Ex. 19:5-6; Lev. 20:24, 26; Deut. 4:8; 7:6-8; 10:14-15; 14:2; 2 Sam. 7:23; 1 Kings 8:53; 1 Chron. 17:21; Amos 3:2; Matt. 10:5-6; 15:24; John 4:22; Rom. 3:2; 16:25-26; Eph. 2:11-19; 3:1-9)

But now, in Christ, *all* who believe are equally the sons of God, one in Christ, and heirs of the blessing of Abraham:

But now in Christ Jesus you who once were far away have been brought near through the blood of Christ. (Eph. 2:13)

This is Paul's simple point in Galatians 3:28: in this great salvation there is no distinction between Jew and Gentile, slave and freeman, male and female. All can equally be saved by faith in Jesus and His death and resurrection. This is the limit of Paul's intention.

In any case, Galatians 3:28 does not abolish all gender distinctions in an *absolute* way because elsewhere Paul gives specific instructions to both men and women. For example:

Now I want you to realize that the head of every man is Christ, and the head of the woman is man, and the head of Christ is God. (1 Cor. 11:3)

Wives, submit to your husbands as to the Lord. For the husband is the head of the wife as Christ is the head of the church, his body, of which he is the Savior. Now as the church submits to Christ, so also wives should submit to their husbands in everything. Husbands, love your wives, just as Christ loved the church and gave himself up for her (Eph. 5:22-25)

The same Paul who wrote, "there is neither... male nor female" also wrote, "the husband is the head of the wife." He was not contradicting himself. His words in Galatians 3 pertain to equality in salvation, while his words in Ephesians 5 pertain to the husband-wife relationship as God has ordained it.

Peter, as we previously noted, observes both realities in his words in 1 Peter 3:1-7 where he affirms that the women are "joint-heirs" with their husbands of "the grace of life," and, at the same time, they are to "be in subjection" to their husbands.[14]

Thus, the Scriptures are quite consistent: they affirm male-female equality as well as male-female role differences. There is no contradiction.

If we are to interpret Paul's words in Galatians 3:28 as abolishing all gender distinctions in an absolute sense, then we would be right to permit people in the church to be homosexuals. Using this very argument, Bible-believing homosexuals claim the right to same-sex relationships because the Bible says "neither male nor female." One influential homosexual writer says, "If there is no longer male and female in Christ Jesus, it does not matter to God which gender we love, which gender we are, or which gender we believe ourselves to be." However, Paul's words in Galatians 3 should be qualified by his other teachings where he describes homosexuality as a sin (e.g., Rom. 1:26-27; 1 Cor. 6:9-10).

Likewise, if Galatians 3:28 meant an absolute abolition of male-female distinctions then it would also abolish slave-master distinctions ("neither slave nor free"). However, Paul elsewhere gave specific instructions to both slave and master as to how they were to conduct themselves in their

---

[14] Quotes here are from the American Standard Version.

particular roles (Eph. 6:5-9; Col. 3:22 – 4:1).[15]

The "Different" Extreme

Here is an example of the "different" extreme:

> Women in 5-fold ministry is a modern phenomena, without
> biblical precedent or historical warrant… In the entire New
> Testament there is not one single example of a woman serving
> in 5-fold ministry!… Early church history lends no support to
> the modern views of qualifying women for ministry office.
> Actually, in the almost 2000 year history of the church women
> never served in ministry office until the last one hundred
> years.[16]

The two passages most commonly used to support this extreme position
are 1 Corinthians 14:34-35 and 1 Timothy 2:11-15.

> *women should remain silent in the churches. They are not allowed*
> *to speak, but must be in submission, as the Law says. If they want*
> *to inquire about something, they should ask their own husbands at*

---

[15] This is not to suggest that slavery is a godly institution (cf. Ex. 21:16; 1 Tim.
1:10, etc.). It was, however, a fact of life in Paul's time and thus he addressed it.
Paul and the other New Testament writers did not defend slavery but simply
instructed believers how to conduct themselves as followers of Jesus Christ in
its midst. It is sometimes argued that just as slavery has been abolished in the
Western world as a result of Christian principles, women should be emancipated
from submission to their husbands. These two institutions, however, are not
comparable. The enduring role distinctions between husband and wife were
instituted by God at the time of creation (Gen. 2:18). Slavery, however, was not
part of the original order of creation. It was a human invention that, like divorce
(Matt. 19:8), God tolerated. Thus, while the New Testament writers gave specific
instructions to slaves, they nowhere defended slavery itself. Quite the opposite:
"if you can gain your freedom, do so" (1 Cor. 7:21). These same writers, however,
affirmed and defended the roles of husband and wife.

[16] Of course, such a statement is grossly inaccurate, both biblically and
historically.

home; for it is disgraceful for a woman to speak in the church. (1 Cor.
14:34-35)

A woman should learn in quietness and full submission. I do not
permit a woman to teach or to have authority over a man; she must
be silent. For Adam was formed first, then Eve. And Adam was not
the one deceived; it was the woman who was deceived and became
a sinner. But women will be saved through childbearing – if they
continue in faith, love and holiness with propriety. (1 Tim. 2:11-15)

At first glance, these passages seem to prohibit women in leadership
or ministry in the church. They appear to state *absolutely* that women
should not teach or even speak in the church. But let's look at each of
them more closely.

1 Timothy 2:11-15

Paul's words in 1 Timothy 2:11-15 are, of course, a matter of great controversy among Christians. One position maintains that vv. 11-12 universally prohibit women from teaching and holding authority over men.
During meetings of the church, women should see their role as that of
the silent learner. Moreover, on the basis of the references to Genesis
in vv. 13-14, such an arrangement is declared by Paul to be absolute,
permanent and universally applicable.

Another position insists that the passage contains a temporary restraining
order issued to curb the activities of a group of women who had been
deceived by the false teachers and were now propagating their heresies
in the church at Ephesus. Thus, Paul's words were specifically occasioned
by, and limited to, what was happening in Ephesus. According to this
position, Paul's instructions were a limited, specific prohibition from
which we may make a general application of principle.

While neither of these positions is entirely free of difficulties, the first
position has by far the most, since, if Paul, in these verses is giving an
absolute and universal prohibition against women leading, teaching or

speaking in the church, then he contradicts other of his own instructions as well as the practices and principles of the early church, as we have previously observed.

It is considerably less problematic to understand Paul's words as a response to local circumstances. In support of this position, there is no question that false teaching at Ephesus prompted Paul to write the book in the first place (1 Tim. 1:3-7; 4:1-8; 6:3-5, 20-21; cf. Acts 20:30). This was not a general "pastoral epistle" as is commonly thought and taught, but it was a specific "apostolic epistle."[17] Paul had left Timothy in Ephesus to set things in order. Timothy was a short-term apostolic delegate with a specific assignment to accomplish in the face of specific abuses and deficiencies of theology and practice in the Ephesian church.

Consequently, Paul's words concerning women in 1 Timothy 2 should not be understood as proceeding from his intention to write some general rules concerning the normative role of women in every church, but rather as a pointed response to specific issues that needed to be addressed at Ephesus. It seems that the false teachers there had found favor in the church among some younger widows, who had opened their homes to them and helped to spread their errors (2 Tim. 3:6-9; 1 Tim. 2:9-15; 5:3-16). Paul now prohibits them from continuing in this.

Such a position is consistent with Paul's practice and teaching elsewhere, as already noted.

However, while acknowledging that local events are the primary occasion for Paul's statements, his references to Creation and the Fall do imply some applicability of his words beyond the limited situation in the Ephesian church. Accordingly, these should be understood to be affirmations of the biblical theme of male leadership, rather than an absolute command that women can never teach or carry any authority.

---

[17] For a verse-by-verse exposition of this book, please see *The Apostolic Epistles #1: A Brief Exposition of 1 Timothy* by Malcolm Webber.

1 Corinthians 14:34-35

Paul's words in 1 Corinthians 14 are harder to understand. They appear to forbid women from speaking in the church, thus contradicting Paul's own words from just three chapters previous (1 Cor. 11:5) as well as elsewhere in his writings.

A variety of explanations has been proposed.

- One explanation is that verses 34-35 are Paul's standard teaching on the normative role of women in the church, and therefore his words in chapter 11 must refer to prayer meetings or some other small group meetings rather than the worship of the whole church. As we have seen, however, there are many passages affirming the appropriateness of women speaking and ministering in the church. Paul surely is not contradicting them all.
- One recent explanation has been that verses 34-35 represent a quotation from the Corinthian believers themselves and that verse 36 is Paul's "indignant reply." While this is a creative idea, there is no real indication of it in the passage.
- A significant number of commentators (including some evangelicals as well as liberals) argue that these verses were added to 1 Corinthians sometime after Paul wrote the letter. This is a relatively easy solution to a difficult problem – simply take the verses out of the Bible!
- The most popular explanation has been that the women at Corinth were involved in disruptive behavior. This scenario proposes that the women sat together on one side of the room with the men on the other and the women were interrupting and shouting questions to their husbands in a disruptive manner. Such an explanation is certainly possible and it is in accord with the immediate context of these two verses: Paul's general call for order in the corporate gatherings of the church in chapter 14. While we do not know if women and men were seated separately in early Christian gatherings or not, this idea

of Paul correcting disruptive behavior (rather than prohibiting any kind of speech) does seem the best choice of interpretations of a difficult passage.

The number of explanations that are suggested for verses 34-35 demonstrates two things.

First, these verses are simply difficult to understand. At face value, they appear to contradict too much of Paul's other writings about women, as well as the rest of the Scripture.

Second, no explanation has been entirely satisfactory. On this side of eternity, we may never know with absolute certainty what these verses mean.[18] In such cases, a spirit of grace and humility is better than one of dogmatic assertion.

As in 1 Timothy 2, it seems that Paul is writing in a local context that we do not fully understand. His words are circumstantially relevant, rather than universally normative in a woodenly-literal way. Clearly he was addressing local situations, rather than attempting to define universal protocols.

Nevertheless, again, as with 1 Timothy 2, there is a universal affirmation of male leadership in this passage ("as the Law says"[19]).

Consequently, while we should not ignore either of these two passages, a wise interpreter will understand them in the context of the entire Bible. We should build our doctrines on the whole Bible and not just on one or two isolated passages, and then interpret difficult passages such as these in view of a balanced doctrine.

---

[18] For an even more difficult passage, please see Paul's words about the "baptism for the dead" in 1 Corinthians 15:29. One commentator has counted nearly two hundred different attempted explanations of that passage!

[19] Significantly, while it is never said in the Law of Moses that women should be silent, the Old Testament does affirm male leadership.

In summary, we should not make these passages absolute. We should not make them our only references on the subject of women in ministry. Then we will avoid the extremes.

Chapter 6

Practical Application

As I have traveled in many nations over the years, a question that repeatedly comes up is, "What is the woman's role in the church?"

Two things are wrong with this:

1. Sadly, this question is rarely asked about the man's role. But it should be. Men are just as prone to getting "out of their roles" as women are, and causing just as much, if not more, damage in doing so.
2. This is the wrong question to ask in the first place. Instead of worrying about "What I can and cannot do," our concern should be "What has God called me to do?"

Instead of trying to build a "wall" around the women to keep them in their place, we should focus on working with both men and women so they will all know their specific positive callings and be released to fulfill them.

This is not to suggest that women will commonly occupy the top leadership roles. As we have seen, it is rare that God calls a woman to a place of top leadership. Deborah and the twelve apostles testify to that, along with the rest of the Bible.

Someone might ask, "But what if God calls a woman to a position of top leadership?" Our answer is that if God calls her to this position, then she had better obey Him and do it.

Another may respond, "Well, what if she just thinks He has called her to this role when He actually hasn't?" Our answer is that this is just as likely to happen with men who err regarding their callings as with women. In both cases, they need to be gently and respectfully corrected and led into their actual callings.

Our primary concern should not be about people getting "out of order," but whether or not they are fulfilling the positive will of God for their lives.

In other words, we should not be so concerned with ensuring that women know what they are *not* supposed to do. Some women will have wrong ideas about their callings just as some men will have wrong ideas about their callings. This is a problem with *both* genders. For both genders, we should encourage the saints to know their callings and fulfill them, and if some people get out of order – either male or female – we should help them on an individual basis to make the necessary adjustments.

This is a healthy, practical approach to the issue of gender and the will of God.

Chapter 7

The Nature of Leadership

"Leadership" does not mean merely being "in charge." There are two sides to leadership, just as there are two sides to a coin: responsibility and authority. You cannot have one without the other.

Thus, the man's call to leadership is a call to *responsibility*. The man is responsible before God in the family, for example, to:

- Love his wife and children unconditionally. Moreover, he should love them with self-giving love, "just as Christ loved the church and gave himself up for her" (Eph. 5:25)!
- Spend time with them.
- Care about them.
- Affirm them.
- Pray for them.
- Protect them.
- Provide for them.
- Teach them.
- Be an example to them.
- Nurture them. [20]

This is true leadership, true servant leadership. It is not merely handing out orders from a high place.

---

[20] For more on the specific roles of husband and wife, and the nature of godly leadership please see *The Christian Family* by Malcolm Webber. For more on leadership and servant leadership, please see books in the *SpiritBuilt Leadership* series by Malcolm Webber.

Leadership is hard. It comes with suffering, self-giving and pain. There is often a high price to be paid to lead. Consequently, not every man desires such responsibility. Many, unfortunately, hide their "talent" in the ground and never embrace their responsibilities (Matt. 25:25). Many men today have become passive, self-serving and unaccountable. They have forsaken their divine calling of leadership and have effectively forsaken their families. Independent, selfish, unaccountable men raise up independent, selfish, unaccountable children who, many times, turn on their own parents; and the cycle continues. God wants this cycle to stop.

When men assume their proper roles as servant leaders in the home and in the church, the women will be delighted to follow them in true submission and many of the common problems caused by women being "out of place" will simply disappear.

Thus, our solution lies not in stopping the women from assuming certain roles, but rather by the men filling the vacuum they had previously left by not fulfilling their God-given leadership roles.

If men will be the leaders God has called them to be, our homes and churches will be healthy and balanced, and both the men and the women will be blessed and fulfilled as we all minister to the fullest extent of our callings in Christ.

A Commentary
on Philippians 4:2-3

The following is taken from Philippians by Gordon D. Fee (Inter-Varsity Press, 1999, pp. 167-171). It represents most of his commentary on Philippians 4:2-3.

In a media-saturated culture like ours, where naming the guilty or the grand is a way of life, it is hard for us to sense how extraordinary this moment is. Apart from greetings and the occasional mention of his coworkers or envoys, Paul rarely ever mentions anyone by name. But here he does, and not because Euodia and Syntyche are the "bad ones" who need to be singled out – precisely the opposite. That he names them at all is evidence of friendship, since one of the marks of enmity in polemical letters is that enemies are left unnamed, thus denigrated by anonymity.

These longtime friends and coworkers, *who have contended at my side in the cause of the gospel,* are no longer seeing eye to eye with each other. We know very little more about them… That Paul had women as coworkers in Philippi should surprise us none, since the church there had its origins among some Gentile women who, as "God-fearers," met by the river on the Jewish sabbath for prayer (Acts 16:13-15). The evidence from Acts indicates that at her conversion Lydia became patron both of the small apostolic band and of the nascent Christian community. By the very nature of things, that meant she was also a leader in the church, since heads of households automatically assumed the same role in the church that was centered in that household. Moreover, Macedonian women in general had a much larger role in public life than one finds elsewhere in the Empire; in Philippi in particular they were also well-known for their religious devotion…

Paul refuses to take sides, thus maintaining friendship with all. He appeals to both women – indeed the identical repetition of their names followed by the verb has rhetorical effect – to bury their differences by adopting the "same mindset." As in the immediately preceding appeal, it is qualified *in the Lord*, evidence that we are not dealing with a personal matter but with "doing the gospel" in Philippi. Having "the same mindset" *in the Lord* has been specifically spelled out in the preceding paradigmatic narratives, where Christ (2:6-11) has humbled himself by taking the "form of a slave" and thus becoming obedient unto death on a cross, and Paul (3:4-14) has expressed his longing to know Christ in a cruciform way...

Paul's erstwhile companion [who he addresses in verse 3 as "loyal yokefellow"] is thus asked to help Euodia and Syntyche, obviously to "be of the same mind" *in the Lord*. It is perhaps significant for our day to note the mediatorial role that Paul's *yokefellow* was expected to play, rather than leaving the two women to work out the problem on their own. Even so, Paul's focus is still on Euodia and Syntyche, not on his yokefellow, and especially, as throughout the letter, their (including the whole community) partnership with him *in the gospel*. His word order tells the story: inasmuch as in the gospel they have contended by my side...

About *Clement and the rest of my fellow workers* we know nothing. The context demands that they are fellow Philippians. Why Paul should single out Clement is a singular mystery, made all the more so by the unusual way the phrase is attached to the former clause, *along with Clement and the rest*. This can only mean that these have also *contended at my side* along with Euodia and Syntyche *in the cause of the gospel* in Philippi. This is probably as close to an "aside" as one gets in Paul's letters. Having just mentioned Euodia and Syntyche in particular, he includes the others who were with him in that ministry from the beginning, for some good reason mentioning Clement in particular, perhaps not wanting to mention the rest by name lest he exclude any. In its own way, therefore, the clause probably functions as a gentle reminder to all who lead the believing community in Philippi to "have the same mindset in the Lord," even though that is not specifically said of or to them...

When the dust clears and one gets beyond the specifics about names and "women in leadership," it is hard to imagine New Testament exhortations that are more contemporary – for every age and clime – than these. To *stand firm in the Lord* is not just a word for the individual believer, as such words are often taken, but for any local body of believers. The gospel is ever and always at stake in our world, and the call to God's people, whose *names are* written *in the book of life,* is to live that life now in whatever "Philippi" and in the face of whatever opposition it is found. But to do so effectively, its people, especially those in leadership, must learn to subordinate personal agendas to the larger agenda of the gospel, "to have the same mindset in the Lord." This means humbling, sacrificial giving of oneself for the sake of others; but then that is what the gospel is all about. So in effect these exhortations merely call us to genuine Christian life in the face of every form of pagan and religious opposition.

At the same time, here is one of those pieces of "mute" evidence for women in leadership in the New Testament, significant in this case for its offhanded, presuppositional way of speaking about them. To deny women's role in the church in Philippi is to fly full in the face of the text. Here is the evidence that the Holy Spirit is gender-blind, that he gifts as he wills. Our task is to recognize his gifting and to assist all such people, male and female, to "have the same mindset in the Lord," so that together they will be effective in doing the gospel.

Books in the *SpiritBuilt Leadership* Series

by Malcolm Webber, Ph.D.

1. *Leadership.* Deals with the nature of leadership, servant leadership, and other basic leadership issues.

2. *Healthy Leaders.* Presents a simple but effective model of what constitutes a healthy Christian leader.

3. *Leading.* A study of the practices of exemplary leaders.

4. *Building Leaders.* Leaders build leaders! However, leader development is highly complex and very little understood. This book examines core principles of leader development.

5. *Leaders & Managers.* Deals with the distinctions between leaders and managers. Contains extensive worksheets.

6. *Abusive Leadership.* A must read for all Christian leaders. Reveals the true natures and sources of abusive leadership and servant leadership.

7. *Understanding Change.* Leading change is one of the most difficult leadership responsibilities. It is also one of the most important. This book is an excellent primer that will help you understand resistance to change, the change process and how to help people through change.

8. *Building Teams.* What teams are and how they best work.

9. *Understanding Organizations.* A primer on organizational structure.

10. *Women in Leadership.* A biblical study concerning this very controversial issue.

11. ***Healthy Followers.*** The popular conception that "everything depends on leaders" is not entirely correct. Without thoughtful and active followers, the greatest of leaders will fail. This book studies the characteristics of healthy followers and is also a great resource for team building.

12. ***Listening.*** Listening is one of the most important of all leadership skills. This book studies how we can be better listeners and better leaders.

13. ***Transformational Thinking.*** This book introduces a new model of transformational thinking – of loving God with our minds – that identifies the critical thinking capacities of a healthy Christian leader. In addition, practical ways of nurturing those thinking capacities are described.

Strategic Press
www.StrategicPress.org

Strategic Press is a division of Strategic Global Assistance, Inc.
www.sgai.org

513 S. Main St. Suite 2
Elkhart, IN 46516
U.S.A

+1-844-532-3371 (LEADER-1)

www.ingramcontent.com/pod-product-compliance
Lightning Source LLC
Chambersburg PA
CBHW071750090426
42738CB00011B/2623